First World War
and Army of Occupation
War Diary
France, Belgium and Germany

28 DIVISION
Divisional Troops
Divisional Signal Company
30 November 1914 - 30 October 1915

WO95/2272/4

The Naval & Military Press Ltd
www.nmarchive.com
Published in association with The National Archives

Published by

The Naval & Military Press Ltd

Unit 10 Ridgewood Industrial Park,

Uckfield, East Sussex,

TN22 5QE England

Tel: +44 (0) 1825 749494

www.naval-military-press.com

www.nmarchive.com

This diary has been reprinted in facsimile from the original. Any imperfections are inevitably reproduced and the quality may fall short of modern type and cartographic standards.

© **Crown Copyright**
Images reproduced by permission of The National Archives, London, England, 2015.

Contents

Document type	Place/Title	Date From	Date To
Heading	WO95/2272/4		
Heading	28th Division Divl Engineers 28th Signals Coy. R.E. Dec 1914-Oct 1915		
Heading	28th Signal Coy. RE Vol II & III 30.11.14-1.3.15 Dec 14 Oct 15		
Heading	War Diary 28th Signal Co		
Miscellaneous	Contents Clothing Chocolate Cigarettes Papers Tin Chicven etc		
War Diary		30/11/1914	30/12/1914
Heading	War Diary 28th Signal Co 31/12/14-31/1/15		
War Diary		31/12/1914	06/01/1915
War Diary	Winchester	07/01/1915	17/01/1915
War Diary	Havre	17/01/1915	17/01/1915
War Diary	Roven	17/01/1915	17/01/1915
War Diary	Serquex	19/01/1915	19/01/1915
War Diary	Abbeville	19/01/1915	19/01/1915
War Diary	Pradelles	20/01/1915	31/01/1915
Heading	1/2/15-1/3/15 War Diary 28th Signal Co		
War Diary	Pradelles	01/02/1915	01/02/1915
War Diary	Vlamertinghe	01/02/1915	01/03/1915
Heading	28th Divl Signal Coy. Vol IV 3-31.3.15		
Heading	Diary March 3rd-31st 1915 28th Div Signal Co. R.E		
War Diary		02/03/1915	31/03/1915
Diagram etc	Circuit Diagram		
Heading	28th Division 28th Signal Coy Vol V		
Heading	War Diary 28th Divl Signal Coy R.E. April 1915		
War Diary	Ypres	01/04/1915	30/04/1915
Heading	28th Division 28th Signal Coy Vol VI		
Heading	War Diary 28th Div Signals Coy R.E. May 1915		
War Diary		05/05/1915	10/05/1915
War Diary	Vlamertinghe	01/05/1915	20/05/1915
War Diary		11/05/1915	14/05/1915
War Diary	Proven	15/05/1915	31/05/1915
Heading	28th Division 28th Signal Coy Vol VII		
Heading	War Diary 28th Div Signal Coy R.E. June 1915		
War Diary	Sheet Square H7c	01/06/1915	01/06/1915
War Diary	Watou	02/06/1915	14/06/1915
War Diary	Westoutre	15/06/1915	30/06/1915
Heading	28th Division 28th Signal Coy Vol VIII		
Heading	Diary 28th Divl Signal Co. July 1915		
War Diary	Westoutre	01/07/1915	31/07/1915
War Diary	Westoutre	01/07/1915	26/07/1915
Heading	28th Division War Diary 28th Divl Signal Coy R.E. August 1915 Vol IX		
War Diary	Westoutre	01/08/1915	31/08/1915
Heading	Mediterranean Expeditionary Force War Diary Unit 28th Div Signal To From 1.9.15 To 30.9.15		
Heading	War Diary Of 28th Divl Signal Co R.E. September 1915		
War Diary	Westoutre	01/09/1915	23/09/1915

War Diary	Merris	23/09/1915	26/09/1915
War Diary	Merville	26/09/1915	26/09/1915
War Diary	Bethune	26/09/1915	27/09/1915
War Diary	Sailly Labourse	28/09/1915	30/09/1915
Heading	Mediterranean Expeditionary Force War Diary Unit 28th Div Signal Co From 1.10.15 To 30.10.15 Volume No. 2		
Heading	War Diary Of 28th Divl Signal Co R.E. October 1915		
War Diary	Sailly Labourse	01/10/1915	06/10/1915
War Diary	Busnes	07/10/1915	23/10/1915
War Diary	Marseilles	24/10/1915	30/10/1915

mom 5095/2272(4)

mom 2222/2(4)

28TH DIVISION
DIVL ENGINEERS

28TH SIGNAL COY R.E.

DEC 1914-OCT 1915

28TH DIVISION
DIVL ENGINEERS

121/4530

28th Signal Coy. R.E.

Vol III & III. 30.11.14 — 1.3.15

Dec '14
Oct '15

30/11/14 — 30/12/14

War Diary

28th Signal Co

Contents
Clothing Chocolate
Cigarette Papers
Tin chicken, etc.

War Diary 28th Divl Signal Coy.   36

Hour Date	Summary of events & information	Remarks
30/11/14 9 am.	Wet. Route march. exercising horses. all sections	
2 pm.	Station practice	
6 pm.	Lamp signalling Lecture	
1/12/14 9 am.	Wet. Cable drill all sections Recruits Gun drill	
3 pm	do Riding drill	
6 pm	Lecture	
2/12/14 9 am.	Wet. Horses exercising 2.3 & 4 sections telephone drill	Recd 3 horses & 2 waggons from Capt Allen U.S.C no harness
3 pm	Preparing for scheme. Instrument testing & cable repairing	
3/12 am.	Fine Left for scheme.	
9.30	BHQ established STREET END. Communication established with Bde HQ & battalions	

Date Hour Place	Summary of Events & Information	Remarks
1 pm	DHQ removed to PETHAM.	Communication
1.30 pm	Signal Office reopened at above.	maintained thro' night 3"-4".
4.12.14	Fine	
8.30 am	Returned DHQ STREET END	
9.15 am	Reopened Signal Office at above	
1 p.m.	CI from all sections	
2.30 pm	Returned to CANTERBURY.	
5.12.14	Fine	
9 am.	Horses exercising	
	Wagons cleaning	
	2, 3 & 4 telephone drill	
6.12.14	Fine	
8.45 am	Divine Service	
7.12.14	Wet.	
9 am.	Recruit drivers Riding instruction	
	Nos 2, 3 & 4 sections Cable drill	
2.30 pm	No 2 Section & HQ recruits	
	moved to 3 St Georges Fields	
6 pm	Lecture.	

Date Hour Rule	Summary of Events Information	Remarks
8.12.14	Wet.	
9 am.	Nos 1.2.3 M+ Cable drill	
3 pm.	Vibrator practice.	
	Cable repairing	
	Harness cleaning	
6 pm	Lecture.	
9.12.14	Wet.	
9 am	No 1.2 3/ Horses Redress route march	
3 pm.	Wagon cleaning + map	
	reading	
10.12.14	Wet.	
9 am	Communication scheme.	
10.30 am	2nd Q. BARHAM	
11.12.14	Fine	
11 am	C.I. from 6 CAMEROON	
11 pm	Rec'd telegram C Force selected for foreign service	
12.11.14	Wet	
9 am	All sections wagon cleaning	
	Horse exercising	

Hour Date Hale	Summary of Events Information	Remarks
13.12.14 8.45 am	Wet Divine service at Cathedral.	
14.12.14 9 am 6 pm	Showery. No 1 Section route march No 2,3,4 Cable drill Vibrator lecture.	
15.12.14 9 am 10.30 am 6 pm	Wet. Dismounted men Route March All horses paraded for inspection by Remount Officer Lecture on vibrator	24 out of 48 considered unfit
16.12.14 9 am 10. am 3 pm	Dull. All sections for route march. Ten men transferred to WINDSOR Vibrator practice.	
17.12.14 9 am	Wet. Sections cable drill 47 horses received from Remounts	

			40

18.12.14	Wet.		
9 am	17 horses recd from Remounts		
12 noon	20 horses sent Reserve Cos. Avs.		
	1 horse died LITTLEBOURNE		
19.12.14	Fine		
9 am	Remounts detached to Sections		
20.12.14	Fine		
8 am	Telegram recd Q480 re Stores in accordance with Sections 28 & 29 G 499.17		
10 am	Wired reply stores in charge portions unserviceable.		
2 pm	Asking reply to Q480. General's 2nd Army.		
2.15 pm	Repeated above.		

3 pm	Msg recd. Central Force asking for statement of unserviceable stores	Q486
21.12.14		
9 am	All horses exercising. Telephone line to WINGHAM repaired.	
3 pm	All stores on cable wagons returned to store for check.	
8 pm	Recd notice of Col Long. inspection of horses @ 10.45 22/12/14	
22.12.14	Fine	
9 am	Horses exercising	
10.45	Inspection horses Col Long.	
11 am	General Heath. inspector of R.E. visit re equipment. Instructed to indent for all required	
3 pm	Wired W.O. for copy G1098.32	
7.30 p	Recd wire C.R.E. 20th Division re officer to report WINCHESTER.	
10 pm	Saw C.R.E. MOORE who phoned WINCHESTER explaining	

1   42

23.12.14	Horses exercising	
9 am		
9.30	Wired C.R.E 28th Division text	S. 46
	confirming phone message.	
	Recd. A. F.S. G. 1098-32 from	
	War Office - + Asst Ordnance.	
	28th Division	
	Ordnance Officer arrived re equipment	
24.12.14	Wet.	
9 am.	Horses exercising	
	Ordnance Officer returned WOOLWICH	
	with indents	
	Recd wire One Officer to report to	
	G.O.C 28th Div. WINCHESTER.	Lt. Parsons.
	Wire recd. Guncotton WOOLWICH re 6 limbered vehicles	
25.12.14	Fine	
9 am	Horses exercising recruits	
	riding instructions	
26.12.14	Wet.	
9 am	Horses exercising	
	Lt. Parsons to WINCHESTER	

1

43

27.12.14	Wet
9 am	Horses exercising. Recruits riding drill.
	Lt Parsons returned.
28.12.14	Wet
9 am	Recruits riding drill.
3 pm	Accoutrements arrived
7 pm	War office saying horses on way.
6 pm	Blankets arrived
~	Clothing arrived
29.12.14	Wet.
9 am	Recruits Riding drill
	Parties at Stations unloading equipment
	Harness & Saddlery arrived
30.12.14	Wet.
9 am	Recruits Riding drill
	Parties at Stations unloading
	Issue of Harness & Saddlery
	Issue Clothing &c.
	Remount Officer called.

3 cable wagons
9 limber wagons
rec'd

31/12/14 – 31/1/15

War Diary

28th Signal Co.

War Diary 28th Divl Signal Co R.E.

31.12.14	Wet.	
9 am	Issue of Harness & Saddlery riding acces.	
3 pm.	Staff Officer visited from 28th Division.	
	Recd wire Central Force asking progress.	Reply S.62
	Wired Woolwich re Stores	S.62a
	Wired Weedon	S.64
	Wired R.C.D.	S.65
1.1.15	Wet.	
9 am	Horses parade in all harness & Saddlery for inspection. A.D.A.D.	
	Wired O 28th Div.	S.66
	" O. Weedon	S.67
	" progress to 28th Div	S.68
3 pm.	Parties unloading stores at Station.	
	Completing issue clothing	
6 pm	Pay.	
9 pm	Notification recd. from WO that unit will proceed WINCHESTER on 5th.	

2.1.15 9 am	Wired Centraforce establishment for Railway move Completed harness issues Wired Ordnance expediting completion	
3.1.15 9 am 11 - 3 pm.	Wet. All horses & vehicles paraded All equipment returned Reissued Clothing & necessaries arrived Recd message to comply with Central Force Order A/30/3/51 6 Horses inspected by V.O Reported unfit for MANCHESTER	Wired for information Nos. 8008 R 8016 R 8035 LD 8102 LD 8096 R 8054 LD

4.1.15	Showery	
9 am	Inspection of all equipment	
	Completing packing	
10 am	~~Kit~~ Ordnance saying Phoned some technical stores still required	
5.1.14	Fine	
5.30	All coy paraded	
7.48	Commenced entraining	
9. am	Entrained	
9.15 am	Left CANTERBURY	
2.40 pm	Arrived WINCHESTER	
4.30 pm	Arrived billets St Cross. Troops billeted St Cross Schools & St Cross Club.	
6.1.14		
9.30	Billeted horses Vet. inspection	
11.45	Attended D.H.Q. D.R.E and Ordnance.	
12.50	Attended D.H.Q. saw C.S.O	
3 pm.	C.S.O visited billets	

WINCHESTER.
7.1.15   Showery
9.30 am   All rifles returned to Ordnance
               WINCHESTER.
               Horses exercising
               One L.D. sent Hospital   8004
3 pm   New rifles drawn from O.O
7 pm   Rifles issued to troops
9 pm   Attended conference
               B.H.Q.

8.1.15   Fine
9.30 am   Troops to CHILCOMBE range
               for musketry.
1.30 pm   Second party to range

9.1.15   Fine
9.30 am   All horses exercised route march
10.30   Remount Officer called
               Major Macfie
2.30   Party to remounts for 10 horses
9 pm   Attended conference B.H.Q.

10.1.15	Wet.	
9.30	Divine Service St. Cross.	
2.15	Medical inspection & inoculation	3 men refused
	Motor lorry & 14 motorcycles arrived	
	2 A.S.C. lorry drivers reported for duty. Armed & equipped	
	Two motorcyclists reported.	
11.1.15	Showery.	
9 am	Meeting on TELEGRAPH HILL re inspection	
	Horses & wagons exercising	
12.1.15	Fine	
7.30 am	Parade for inspection by H. Majesty	
9.30 am	Arrived position on FARLEY DOWN	
10.40 am	H. Majesty arrived	
1.15 pm	Returned.	
3 pm	Issued Identity discs.	
	Read ...... to Convoy reforming on Wednesday.	

13.1.15	Fine	
9. am	Field Dressing & Iodine issued	
9.30	Horses & wagons exercising	
	Bde sections telephone drill	
14.1.15	Fine	
9 am.	Completing packing equipment	
10	Received instructions re embarkation	
15.1.15	Fine	
9 am.	Paraded marched to SOUTHAMPTON.	
11 am.	Passed point 1 m. N of COMPTON.	
3 pm.	Arrived docks.	
5 pm.	Completed embarkation	
6 pm.	Sailed	
16.1.15	Very windy & stormy	
11.30 pm	Arrived HAVRE	
	Disembarked	
17.1.15		
8 am	Marched to Point 1.	
	GARE MERCHANDISE	

HAVRE 19.4.15		
10.30 am	Sufficient train accommodation not available. No 2 detachment complete with vehicles & horses – also motorcar. Three G.S. & one cable wagon (less horses) sent.	2 cable wagons 1 water cart 1 limb. G.S. 16 NCO's & men 17 horses.
4 pm	Interviewed D.A.T.D. received instructions bivouac for night in Station Yard.	
HAVRE 11.30 am	Fine & cold. Received instructions from DAA TMG to entrain GARE MARITIME at 9 pm.	
3 pm.	Instructions altered by DART. to entrain Point 1 at 7.30 pm.	
6 pm	Commenced entraining	
11 pm	Left HAVRE	
ROVEN. 2.40 am.	Arrived	Left Sergt. Creston to report A.G.
3.25	Resumed journey	

51

19.1.15

SERQUEX.
6.20 am

6.53 am

Dull. Snow in places
Arrived
Horses watered & fed
Resumed journey.

ABBEVILLE
19.1.15
12.50 pm.

1.38 pm

Arrived.
Horses watered & fed.
Hot tea supplied troops
Resumed journey.

PRADELLES.
20.1.15
9 am
10 am

3.27 pm

10.20 pm.

Showery
Received instructions to Signal Office
Took over Signal Office
Bare board set & three men
working 5th Corps. HAZEBROUCK
    27th Division
    2nd Corps
Established Vibrator line to
80th Brigade
Established   do.
83rd Brigade

PRADELLES.   Wet.
21.1.15.
7 p.m.   Established office to 85th Brigade
                CAESTRE
                Parsons went to 1st Division
                Gunners of 1st Signal Coy arrived

PRADELLES.   Fine
22.1.15.   Three vibrator offices working to
                83. 84. 85 Brigades.
                Three detachments out wheres
                poling same.

PRADELLES.   Fine
23.1.15   Three lines to bdes.
                83rd & 84th on Commutator.
                85th on single
                Corps line made direct to E.C.O

PRADELLES.   Fine
24.1.15   In communication with
                     three brigades as yesterday
10. am.   Signals from O.C.D removed
                     2nd class office & substituted ditto
                     as continuing line to CAESTRE
11 am.   M.H.R. 2d Corps called. Went
                     with him to CAESTRE visited
                     Bde section office – also office
                     of Corps at railhead
4 pm.   Superimposed vibrator on air
                     line between PRADELLES and
                     CAESTRE. Bde section running
                     cable to her line from Bde HQ.

PRADELLES.   Fine
25.1.15
9 am   Visited position to be taken
                     by division with Maj. Maofie.
                     In communication with three
                     brigades. Corps H.Qrs & CAESTRE
                     station.
                     ZHD came on line FB11 & ZAC

PRADELLES.
26.1.15   Fine
9 am   Line to ZHD reeled up.
              Two vibrators working with
              3 bdees. Two on line YBH.ZHC
              time on Corps line to railhead
12 noon   Adams returned to 1st Div.
1 pm   Parsons returned
3 "   OaS visited Office.
10.15 pm   Operator (Corps) noticed repeating
              messages indifferent work.

PRADELLES.   Fine
27.1.15
9 am   Good Signals all Stations
10.15 am   Operators of Corps exchanged
10.45 am   Line YBH to CR changed
              over to new line

PRADELLES.   Fine
28.1.15
9 am   Signals good.
11 am   Line YBH. reported line requiring
              attention between YBH & CR.
              Informed CR. asked send linesman
              to assist.

PRADELLES.   Fine   55
29.1.15
9 am   Signals good.
              Circuit to 28th
11 am   Dis on CR line.
2.15pm   Signals good
3.0pm   Rearranged wires to B.CO al.
6 pm   Signals weak + unintelligible
              line CR & B.CO
9.30pm   Connected thro' telephone to
              B.CO for G.OC to speak.

PRADELLES.
30.1.15   Fine
9 am.   Signals good.
11.30.   Visited 5th Div. to see lines
4 pm   Returned

PRADELLES.   Snowing.
31.1.15.
9 am.   Signals good.
7 pm.   No 1 Section marched to VLAMERTINGHE

1/2/15 — 1/3/15

War Diary

28th Signal Co

War Diary 28th Divl Signal Co R E 56

PRADELLES

Fine

9 am. Closed Signal Office & moved
VLAMERTINGHE to VLAMERTINGHE
4 pm - 1/7/15 Laid cable from BRANDHOEK
to junction on YPRES - Vlamertinghe
Ypres - a[t] junction.
Laid line to 83rd Bde, r.h.a.
Signals good.

2/7/15
8.30 am. D[itt]o on 83rd Line
4.30 Signals good

7 pm Line laid to 84th Bde.
part Railway line used.

3/7/15. Fine
Sig. good
Communication by wire to
85th Bde. BASSE BOOME
Railway line used.

4/7/15 Fine
Extensions to all lines being
made for transference of Sig Office
to YPRES.
One hour's disconnection on line
84th brigade during night 4 - 5

57

5.2.15	Fine
9 am	All lines arranged for at YPRES and POPERINGHE to change Signal Office
1.30 pm	Instructions given alteration DHQ to Chateau — all lines continued from existing office to here. New lines to YPRES disconnected forward.
4 pm	Signal Office reopened at Chateau

6.2.15	Fine
9 am	Signals good.
11.30	Dis in line ZHD intermediate line ZHD to ZHC.
2 pm	Through.
4 pm	Two clear lines working Communication one cable line to ZHE
6 pm	ZHE closed office — they marching to YPRES.
11.30 pm	General Staff to POPERINGE for night.

7.2.15. Lines to Bde HQrs duplicated
Signals good

8.2.15. ~~Line across~~
Reserve line to 84th Bde run
also cross line to 85th

9.2.15 Rearranged all leading in Cables.
Sigs good.

10.2.15 Conducted Lt Cols. Leigh & Rowell
round communications
Sigs good

11.2.15 Bde sections improving their
lines – 4 miles cable sent them.
Signals good

12.2.15 Lines across roads at HQrs.
carried higher –
Signals good

13.2.15 Fine
All lines disced at 83rd by
shell fire -
Repaired all O.K.

14.2.15 Wet. Sigs O.K.
~~Extra~~ Extra lineman &
cable loaned Bde Section

15.2.15 Wet.
Signals O.K.

16.2.15 Fine.
Parson at R.C.
4 drums cable to Bde Section
Continuing line to YPRES for
telephone to Commandant. Tried
Six telegraphists arrived from
GHQ.
Complaints made reference lines
to trenches - Asked if lead
covered cable could be supplied

Promised 5 W.T. from 5th Corps.
" Telephones + Exchange }
from 5th Divl Coy }

17.2.15.	Wet. Sigs good R.C. Q and Bdes. Commn good on left section even lines to trenches Lines Bdes to bttns on right Section maintained. impos̄ to get to trenches	Visited right section. Reported to GS(I).
18.2.15	Wet Sent to bed by MO orders. Sig. good. Lines to Bdes & trenches on left section good. Trench lines to right Section commenced again	
19.2.15	Fine Sick	
20.2.15	Fine Sick	

21.2.15	Fine
	Telephone cable line R.V.B.H
	to Administrative completed
	French civil phones used
	Speaking good
	Telephone R.C to C.R.E
	completed. Speaking good
	9th Bde took over right section
	and bde section replaced
	No 3 section until 25th.
	No 4 section with 13th Bde
	took over left section from
	83rd bde.
	No 2 section at rest camp
	BUSSEBOOM.
10 pm	Dis on line Z 1.
11 pm.	Commn re-established
	Four motorcyclists arrived
	from BASE

22.2.15 Fine

Line laid from permanent line
VLAMERTINGHE to H+a

Above line continued to
BUSSEBOOM

Common opened.

RC closed 7.45 pm.

All other lines & common good

Lines to trenches in both
sections good. Disconnections
during day repaired each
night.

Still great difficulty maintaining
right section trench lines
impossible to do any work
by daylight

23.2.15	Fine
Sigs good throughout night
RC opened 10.30 am
Visited Bde Hrs & Cavalry
HQ with Sig OCO
All lines maintained
RC closed 8.10 pm
24.2.15	Snow. rain
Signals good
RC opened 10 am
Altered Cmdts YPRES telephone
line to 84 Rue de Lille

Cut back all forward or
hanging telephone lines out
of YPRES

Informed that 4th detachment
of Wos Section leaving ~~England~~
ABBEVILLE today

Line to 9th Bde dis at 1pm
Reserve line in use until 2pm
Line restored |

25.2.14	Fine
	Signals good
	Cut away Railway lines S.E of
	YPRES recovered $\frac{3}{4}$ mile old
	disused cable running E
	on railway with inductive Sig.
	on.
	Ran leads from old wires to
	test box at 100 yards distance
	from R.E.
26.2.14	Fine
	Construction parties running
	separate telephone lines to two
	forward brigades
	One Officer 22 men 3 vehicles
	2 horses composing 4th det.
	arrived
	All comms maintained
	French lines repaired during
	night

7.2.14	Line
	Completed telephone circuits
	and all connected to Field
	exchange
	All lines & signals maintained
28	
8.2.14	Line
	R.C. opened at 9.30 am
	Recovered two spare lines to YPRES
	L. Kirby exchanged duties with
	L. Emery with No 3 section
	R.C. closed 5.55 pm.
	All lines maintained.
	Trunk lines repaired during
	night.
3.15	Storms.
	Signals all good.
	R.A. office added to telephone ex.
	Trunk lines R/BN & T/BN dis
	all night - working in POPERINGHE
	All other lines maintained
	except trunk lines to right
	section by shell fire

28th Div¹ Signal Coy.

Vol IV 3 - 31. 3. 15.

Diary
March 3rd – 31st 1915

28th Div. Signal Co. R.E.

2.3.15	
3.15	Fine
	Signals good
	Phone line Y Bry & R/X Bry.
	restored 11.30 am
	R.C. open 10.30 am
	Phone line to Brigades down
	one hour restored 11.30 am
	Commenced recasting Artillery
	lines to Brigades
	R.C. closed 7.30 pm
3.3.15	
3.14	Rain
	Signals good
	Reconstructing Artillery lines
	All trench lines to right section
	S of canal blown to pieces
	Line laid joining left trench
	of 27th Div to right of 28th.
	All other lines reconstructed
4.3.15	
3.15	Fine
	Lines S of canal again destroyed
	after repairs during night
	men of batta section all worn out
	Two disconnections to telephone
	line and one to vibrator line
	to Brigade 15 by Searchers

68

4th
2.15   Lines repaired Commn good.

No 2 Section relieved No 3 Section
in right sector

5th
2.15   Fine

All lines with exception trench
lines S of canal good

Signals good.

Every effort being made during
darkness to reinstate trench
lines S of canal

6th
3.15   Wet
All divisional lines good
Brigade lines to bastion damaged
reserve lines used during night

Efforts to reinstate trench lines
S of canal failed with casualties

All others repaired

2.15 Nil.

Signals good + commn maintained
with exception trench lines S of
Canal.

Diagram to date.

[diagram]

8/3/15
15
True
Signals good
Trench lines S of canal replaced
during night. diagram above
Nos. 26. 27. 28.
All other commn maintained

9 3.15	Fine	
9 am	All lines maintained Signals good. Trench line 26 dissed during night & repaired	
11.25am	Report centre open	
8.45pm	Ditto closed Sigs good.	
10 3.15	Fine & dull	
	All lines maintained & Sigs good.	
10 am	R.C. opened	
11 am	All trench lines S. of canal dissed by shell fire	
7.30pm	R.C. closed. Sigs good.	
11.3.15	Fine	
9 am	All lines maintained Sigs good. Trench lines 28 & 27 & dressing station S. of canal repaired during night. Main cross line between bdes dissed reserve wire in use.	
10.30am	R.C. opened	
10.40am	Cross line between bdes repaired	

3 pm	All trench lines N half of Left section ceased by shell fire
4 pm	One trench line of above repaired
7 pm	R.C. closed.
7.30 pm	Cable detachment laid line 65th How. to VIERSTAAT as observation post
11.40 pm	Trench lines 38 39 43 46 50 repaired & new line laid to 38
12.3.15	Fine but dull
9 am	All lines maintained sigs good
10.30 am	RC opened
6.10 pm	Trench lines 27.28 S of canal dis — new line to advance post of Dressing station S of canal laid
8.15 pm	R.C. closed.
13.3.15	Fine
9 am	All lines maintained & sig. good except lines S of canal all dis
10.30 am	RC opened
8.15 pm	RC closed.

14.3.●	Fine
10.15 am	Report centre opened
	All lines maintained & signals good
	except trench line "74 dis'ed at
	8 am
5 pm	Very heavy shell fire
6.15 pm	All trench lines S. of canal dis'ed
	also duplicate line to Bastn HQ
6.20 pm	Reserve line to Right Bde dis
8.30 pm	Ditto repaired
	RC open all night
	All Div'l to Bde lines maintained
15.3.15	Fine dull
	Signals good
10 am	Telephone lines to both bdes dis'ed
11 am	Ditto to bdes. repaired
10.10 am	Right bde report all lines good.
3 pm	Heavy shell fire
5.10 pm	Main line right bde dis'ed
	reserve line in use
5.20 pm	Both bde phone lines dis'ed
6.8 pm	Left bde report all forward lines
	good.
6.30 pm	New line thro' YPRES to right
	bde completed
7.30 pm	Phone lines repaired
8 pm	RC closed.

20.3.15	Lines
9 am	All lines maintained. Sigs good
10.15	R.C. opened
12	Both phone lines to bdes dissed
1.10 pm	Ditto repaired
7.30 pm	R.C. closed.
21.3.15	Lines
9 am	All lines maintained Sigs good
10.15 am	R.C. opened
1 pm	Both lines to P.O.P. diss.
1.30 pm	Both lines to Left Bde diss also phone lines to both bdes & one line to Right Bde. using reserve line to Right Bde
1.50 pm	Commn with Left Bde established thro R. Bde by X line
2 pm	One line to POP repaired
2.30 pm	Both lines to R. bde through.
2.45 pm	Reserve line to L bde repaired
3.10 pm	Both lines to PoP through.
3.30 pm	Phone line to L. Bde repaired
6 pm	All lines through.
6.30 pm	Phone to L Bde diss
6.45 pm	Ditto repaired
7.40 pm	R.C. closed
8.15 pm	New phone line Reslerg Bde through

16.3.●	Fine
9 am	All lines maintained Sigs good
10.45 am	RC opened
3.15 pm	Phone line to POP. dissed at VLAMER
3.30 pm	Ditto repaired
8.50 pm	RC closed.
17.3.15	Fine dull
9 am	All lines maintained Sigs good
10.15 am	RC opened
	Quiet day
7.25 pm	RC closed.
18.3.15	Fine dull
9 am	All lines maintained Sigs good
10.15 am	RC opened
3 pm	Line from RE to balloon run
6.45 pm	RC closed.
19.3.15	Showers & wind
9 am	All lines maintained Sigs good
10.15 am	RC opened
7.15 pm	RC closed.

22.3●	Fine
9 am	All lines maintained Sigs good
10.5	RC opened
7.57pm	RC closed
	Class of 30 Infantry commenced
	POP & class to Artillery at R. Centre
23.3.15	Cloudy & dull
9.0 am	All lines maintained Sigs good
9.45 am	RC opened
11.30 am	Changed phone line to POP into airline
1.30 pm	Contact on Vet line Left Bde & their phone.
7.54pm	RC closed
8 pm	Contact cleared.
24.3.15	Dull showery
9 AM.	All lines maintained Sigs good
10.40 am	RC opened
8.39 am	Right Bde lines OK
9.12 am	Left Bde lines OK.
	Moved wireless listening station to YPRES.
7.45 pm	RC closed

25.3.15	Wet.
8.35 am	Right bde report sigs OK.
9 am	Divl sigs OK
9.55 am	Left bde report sigs OK
10.30 am	R.C. opened
3 pm	Returned wireless listening station to RC reopened.
7.45 pm	RC closed.
26.3.15	Dull
8.40 am	Right bde report sigs OK & duplicate line run from Battn HQ to 34 trench
9 am	Divl sigs OK
9.40 am	Left bde report sigs OK
10.30 am	RC opened.
3 pm	New set wireless for listening station received & fixed up.
8.45 pm	RC closed.
27.3.15	Fine
9 am	Divl sigs OK
9.5 am	Right bde report Sigs OK
11.28 am	Left bde report Sigs OK. Fixing up direction finding wire to wireless listening station

7.37		R.C. closed.
28.3.15		Fine
9 am		Divl Sigs. OK.
8.10 am		Right bde report sigs. OK.
9.53 am		Left bde report sig. OK
4 pm		F1 (suspect stn.) heard calling on wireless listening station
6.30 pm		Report C. closed.
29.3.15		Fine
8.57 am		Right bde report sig. OK
9 am		Divl sigs OK
9.15 am		Left bde report sig. OK
9.30 am		Left bde telephone line dis
10.15 am		ditto repaired
		F1 (suspect stn.) heard on wireless wave obtained 145 metres. rough direction due E
6.15 pm		Right bde. report line to 26 trench dis others OK
7.30 pm		R.C. closed.
10.2 pm		Right bde report line to 26 trench repaired Sig. OK.

30.3	Fine	
9 am	Divl sigs. OK	
9.30	ZV heard calling on wireless listening station reading	Results given to G.S.
9.17am	Left bde report sigs OK	
10 am	Right bde report sigs OK	
6 pm	Unknown Station heard on wireless. No station call (Code) Attempt to localise failed	
7.43pm	R.C. closed.	
31.3.15	Fine	
7 am	F1 heard on wireless Stn until 7.50 unable to hear on to localise. F1 immediately stopped no sigs heard after aeroplane started.	Results given to G.S.
7.50 am	FG also heard – stopped when aeroplanes about.	
9 am.	Divl lines OK	
9.2 am	Right bde report sigs OK except	trench 32 B.
10.10 am	Left bde report Sigs OK	
11.35 am	Main line to Right Bde dis	
2.20 pm	Ditto repaired	
7.50 pm	R.C. closed	
midnight	Number messages for day R.C. 179 HQM. & G.S. 273	

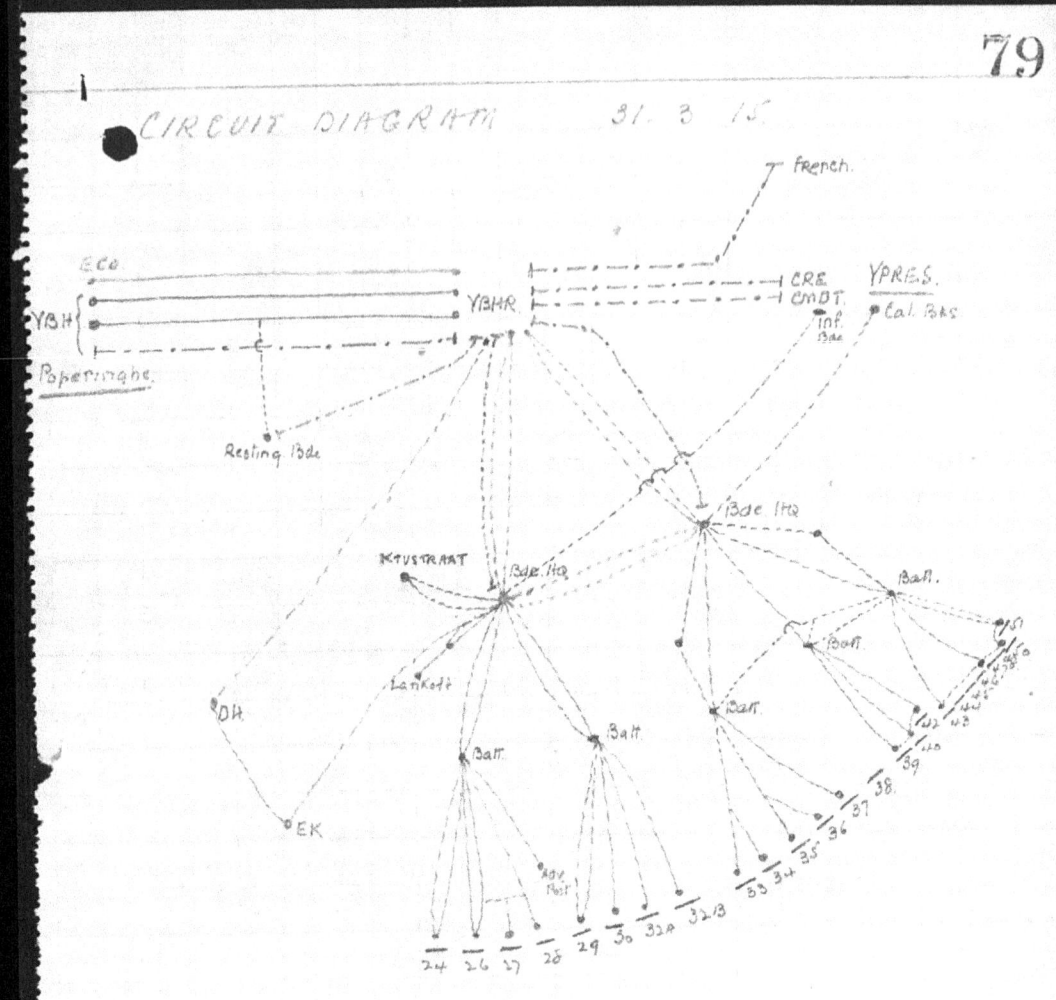

121/6306

28th Division

28th Signal Cor

V

Secret

War Diary

28th Divl Signal Co R.E.

April 1915

YPRES

1.4.15	Fine
8.40 am	~~Left~~ bde report sigs. OK.
9.0 am	Divl Sigs OK
10.12 am	~~Right~~ bde report sig. OK. except 27 trench dis
11.25 am	Main line dis Reserve line in use
1 pm	do OK.
7.41 pm	R C closed.
	Total messages { Report centre 229
	dealt with { Poperinghe 277

2.4.15.	Fine
9 am	Divl lines OK.
9.10 am	Left Bde report OK.
9.26 am	Right Bde report OK
11.0 am	Wireless listening station removed to POTIJZE and fixed up with listening wire.
7.57 am	RC closed.
	Total messages { Report centre 259
	dealt with { Poperinghe 279

3.4.15	Dull Showery.
8.40 am	Left bde report line to middle battn dis others OK.
8.41 am	Right bde report OK
9 am	Divl lines OK
11.10 am	Second line to POPERINGHE dis but correct to Resting Bde.
11.56 am	Sigs to POP. OK.
6.30 pm	Line to 2g trench dis
8.15 pm	RC closed
9.10 pm	Line to 2g trench repaired
	Total messages } Report Centre 266.
	dealt with } POPERINGHE 253

4.4.15	Showery
8.41 am	Right bde report OK
9 am	Divl lines OK
9.30 am	Left bde report OK.
3 pm	No 2 section left to rejoin 83rd Bde at WESTOUTRE — 15th Bde section having arrived
7.35 pm	RC closed.
9.35 pm	Phone line to POP. dis
10.30 pm	Ditto repd VLAMERTINGHE — Shell fire
	Messages dealt { Report Centre 215
	with { Poperinghe 278

		82

5.4.15 — Wet.
7.59am — Right bde report OK.
9 am — Divl Sigs OK.
12.50pm — Both lines PoP. dis.
1.5 pm — Left bde report OK except trench line 35 dugouts & lines destroyed by trench mortar

        Messages dealt with PoP 210
                            R C 326

6.4.15 — Wet
9 am — Divl Signals good
9.5 am — Bdes report sigs OK
3 pm — Handed over all lines to 5th Div. These lines tested through from PoP. to new R C YPRES & commn opened. Retained intermediate office in 5th Div. line to Lieut VLAMERTINGHE

7.4.15 — Fine
9 am — Detachment at YPRES leading in 3 new lines from VLAMERTINGHE to R.C. Signal office opened R C YPRES D.R's doing local circulations
11.30am — Interview with 37th French div. & obtained diagram
NOON — Fixed up phone GS to PoP

	Messages dealt with 319
8.4.15	Showery
9 am	Signals with R C OK
	Phone lines established to R C
	with C R E on exchange
10 AM	Commenced line to R bde
	Three lines carried on line being
	laid fd from RC to bde HQ
1 pm	Right bde report lines OK
9.5 pm	PZ temporary office on R. bde
	line Sigs OK
9.4.15	Showery
1.14 AM	Line to right bde complete & commn
	established
	Messages 513
8 AM	All lines div between R.C & POP
9.15 am	Sigs OK
10 AM	Detachment running L Bde line
	completed as far as NEILTZE
	Messages AQ 266
	RC 109 = 375
10.4.15	Fine
9 am	Sigs to AQ & ZItC (R bde) good
	Reserve line to ZItC completed
3 pm	R.C opened
6 pm	L Bde moves ST Jean. intermediate
	Sigs OK
7 pm	L Bde OK

	Completed construction 2 air lines to VERLORENHOEK	
	Messages dealt with RC 155	
	HQ 367	= 522
11/15	Dull	
9 am	Arol lines OK	
9.30 am	L bde report OK	
10 am	R A line construction continued	
3 pm	bde line to AQ dis	
3.30 pm	Sigs OK	
5 pm	Commn established with 27th Div.	
7.30 pm	All RH bde lines completed	
	Messages dealt with RC 267	
	HQ 333	= 600
12/15	Dull	
8 am	Sigs OK	
9 am	R bde report OK	
9.30 am	L bde report two battns dis	
9.45 am	L bde report one battn OK	
5 pm	L bde report OK	
5.30 pm	Reserve lines to both bdes tested	OK
	Messages dealt with RC 236	
	HQ 321	= 557
13/15	Fine	
9 am	Sigs OK	
9.8 am	R bde report OK	
11.7 am	L bde report OK except line R battn dis	
1 pm	All bde lines & RA lines on single circuits with bde lines duplicated	

	Messages dealt with HQ 338	
	RC 404 =	742
14.4.15	Fine	
9 am	All lines OK	
	Messages dealt with HQ 362	
	RC 447 =	809
15.4.15	Fine	
9 am	Divl lines OK	
9.15 am	R bde report OK except L battn dis & since repaired	
9.20 am	L bde report OK	
1 pm	Reserve bde came on spare line from VLAMERTINGHE	
2 pm	New lines to 85th Bde completed	
2.30 pm	Reserve bde ceased from VL.	
11.50 pm	84th Bde took over from 85th who opened new office VLORENHOEK	
midnight	Messages dealt with HQ 343	
	R.C 494 =	837
16.4.15	Fine	
2.5 am	85th Bde opened office in new position	
9 am	Sigs OK	
	Messages dealt with HQ 330	
	RC 465 =	795

86

17.4.15 9am	Fine Sigs OK all round Messages dealt with AQ 353 RC 565 = 918	
18.4.15 9am 11am	Fine Sigs OK all round New lines being run for AQ to VLAM. Messages dealt with AQ 387 RC 478 = 865	
19.4.15 9am 6pm	Fine Sigs OK all round New signal office AQ all complete Messages dealt with AQ 378 RC 551 = 929	
20.4.15 9am 9.30am 9.27am 3pm 5pm	Dull Sigs OK Signal office removed to VLAMERTINGHE – 5th Corps RC open 85th Bde Sigs OK 83rd & 84th Bdes Sigs OK 3 detachments marched to VLAMERTINGHE All lines through to Chateau Messages dealt with AQ 315 RC 406 = 721	

21.4.15	Fine	
9 am	83rd Sig. OK	
7.46 am	84th Sig. OK	
9.56 am	80th Sig. OK	
11 am	Base Office POPERINGHE closed & reopened VLAMERTINGHE chateau	
12.30 pm	Remainder Coy moved to new billet	
3 pm	A.C. at YPRES closed & office opened VLAMERTINGHE chateau	
	Messages dealt with Q. 510	
	R.C. 364 672	

22.4.15	Fine	
11 am	All communication OK	
5 pm	Heavy attack and YPRES shelled	
7 pm	2 bde lines dis	
8 pm	All bde lines dis	
	Messages to bdes by OR	
	Bdes report passed wires OK	
	Communication maintained to H.Qrs Canadians and 27th Divisions	

23.4.15	Fine	
	Sig. maintained to Cdns & between 27th Div. All bde lines dis	
	Working parties working on same all night	
	Short periods of lines bde to bdes	
	All messages by OR	

88

24.4.15	Fine
9am	Bde lines that Div & Bdes OK
	Heavy shelling & fighting
	Bdes report by DR forward lines OK
	Messages by DR all day
7pm	Party under Lt LYCETT laid new line
	to R. bde
1am	Sigs to right bde OK
1.30am	" " "

25.4.15	Fine
9am	Bde lines, div & others OK
	Bde lines forward OK
	Rather our repairing lines
2.30pm	Party under Lt LYCETT new line to
	bde
	Communication with 8th Corps Lahore
	Canadian & 27th Divisions OK
	Q office removed to POPERINGHE
	Messages sent 85th bde hrs took bde
	of 27th div.

26.4.15	Fine after rain last night
7am	Lt LYCETT & Sapper Reeves reported
	wounded – new line at change
9am	Report from 85th bde lines all for lines
	OK. Stay other also.

89

26.4.15	contd Telegraph & telephone communication maintained with 5th Corps, Canadian Lahore & 27 Div.
	All R.A. lines & CRE Lahore Div. OK
	Bdes obtained through 27th Div
	Parties out repairing lines
2 pm	Parties returned. Temporarily address only
7 pm	New line being laid
27.4.15	Quiet
2 am	Party reached MENIN gate only impossible to proceed
4 am	Other lines as yesterday. OK
10 am	Party again on line
4 pm	Sigs to 5th Corps. All lines to 2nd R.C.
8.15 pm	Sigs to 85th OK lines to B rdy
28.4.15	True
1.15 am	Bde line dis
4 am	Another comms maintained
3 pm	Parties on Bde lines — west station established railway crossing MENIN road
6.20 pm	Bde line OK
6.30 pm	Bde line dis

29.4.15	Fine
9 am	Bde line dis - others maintained
2.30 pm	83rd Bde line OK & to 83rd & 84th
4.10 pm	Bde line dis
7.30 pm	ditto OK
8.30 pm	again dis

30.4.15	Fine misty early morning
9 am.	Line to Bde still dis linesmen out. Parties both ends running new line Commun PLUMERS FORCE R.C by telephone vibrator and to ABEELE by D.C set also 27th & Lahore Div. & 83, 84 & 85th Bdes two PF
10 am.	Line laid across to Canadian Div.
4.30 pm	Sigs to Bdes OK.

121/6306.

28th Division

28th Signal Coy
no six

Secret.

War Diary

    28th Divl Signal Co R.E

        May 1915.

5.5.15	Fine	
9.30am	R.C moved to Square H 7c	
	Sigs OK	
	Constant [breakages] on bde lines	
10 pm	Commn opened with Administration Staff PROVEN	Message 407
6.5.15	Fine	
9 am	Sigs OK	
3.20pm	D.C set vibrator on to ABEELE	
4.20pm	Above OK	Message 377
7.5.15	Fine Heavy Shelling	
9 am	Sigs OK	
	Constant breakages to bde lines. Others OK.	Message 401
8.5.15	Fine	
	Constant breakages to bde lines but Communication kept going. Others OK.	Message 429
9.5.15	Fine	
	As day before.	Message 416
10.5.15	Fine	
	Sigs and bdes Constant breaking Others OK	Message 392

1.5.15 VLAMERTINGHE	Fine	
	Line to Bdes dis. others OK	
2 am.		
11.45 am	Line to bdes OK	
4.25 pm	do dis	Messages
5 pm	L. MOORSHEAD reporty arrived from II Army	415
2.5.15	Fine	
2.40 am	Lines to Bdes OK. others OK	
6.30 pm	Bde line dis	
	Cavalry wireless station working from VERLORNHOEK to VLAMERTINGHE	Messages
7.25 pm	Line to Bdes OK	425
3.5.15	Fine	
12.30 am	Bde line dis	
2 am	do OK	
9 am	Sigs OK	
	Constant breakages of bde lines this day but commn maintained	Messages 377
4.5.15	Fine	
9 am	Sigs OK	Messages
	Continual breakage of bde lines others OK	412

16.5.15	Fine	
6am	Maj. H.C. Saunders to England on leave.	
9am	Sigs OK.	
17.5.15	Fine	
	Sigs OK	
18.5.15	Fine	
	Sigs OK	
19.5.15	Fine	
	Sigs OK	
	19 men reinforcements reported HQ.	
	Lt. PARSONS to ENGLAND on leave.	
	MAJ. Saunders returned.	
20.5.15	Fine	
	Sigs OK	
9am	Reinforcements sent to bde sections	
11.30am	Took over Offices at R.C. H.Q. from 85th bde.	
3pm	Completed power lines to CAV DIV	
	rearranged lable over N lines –	
	Commn established to 83rd Bde west	
	Camp, G5d	
8pm	Line hrs to 85th Bde POTIZE	Message 3/6
	Sigs OK.	

94

11.5.15 9 am	Fine All sigs OK. Constant breakages of bde lines	Message 417
12.5.15	Fine As any before.	Message 389
13.5.15 9 am 4 pm	Fine Sigs OK R.O. closed. reopened PROVEN. Bdes moving back to rest.	
14.5.15 9 am.	Nes. Bde lines handed over to CAV. CORPS. RA remain with them. Laid lines to WATOU, WINIZEELE and HERZEELE to connect bdes. DHQ at PROVEN Composite bde at VLAMERTINGHE Communn thro' 5th Corps, also RA	
PROVEN 15.5.15	Fine Sigs OK Reported DAG Base. 23 men required to complete.	

25.5.15	Fine
9 am.	Sigs OK 83rd 84th & 85th Bdes.
5 pm.	8th Bde intermediate on S. Line
	new poled cable line laid from
	YBHR to best station S.T.
6 pm	84th Bde to rest camp.
	Messages dealt with 616.
26.5.15	Fine
9 am.	Sigs OK. 84th 85th 80th & 8th Bdes.
10 am	new airline built to S. Line
9 pm	Sigs OK
10 pm	8th Bde on forward line
	Messages dealt with 572
27.5.15	Dull & windy
9 am	Sigs OK
	85th & 8th Bdes on forward lines
	84th Bde at rest camp.
3 pm.	S.T. office opened in H 11 b for
	Divl reserve & 151st Bde.
28.5.15	Fine windy NE
9 am	All sigs OK.
9.35 pm	9th Bde came in line to 85th
12 am	85th off relieved by 9th.

21.5.15	Fine	
6 am	Took over line to 86th bde from CAV.	
8 am	Sig OK	
10.15 am	R.C opened	
9 am	Line laid to POPERINGHE to pick up R.C.	
	Sigs dis to 86th at intervals	
1.15 pm	Line to PROVEN through.	Message
6.30 pm	RC closed	452.
22.5.15	Fine	
9 am	Sig OK	
	Sigs to 86th intermittent	Message
6 pm	R.C closed	427
23.5.15	Fine	
9 am	Sig OK	
6 pm	RC closed.	
	3 detachments at R.C. one detachment	Message
	+ HQ section PROVEN.	409.
24.5.15	Fine	
2.30 am	Very heavy shelling Sig RC OK	
	Bde line dis	
9 am	Sig OK	
2 pm	84th bde thro' on Scrub line	Message
5 pm	80th bde ditto	438.

97

29.5.15	Fine	
9 am	Sigs OK to 8th & 9th Bdes. &	
	84th & 85th in rest.	
30.5.15	Fine	
9 am	Sigs OK	
	Attended conference 2nd Army Signals	
31.5.15	Fine	
9 am	Sigs OK	
3 pm	Sigs 6th Divn arrived	
11 pm	18th Bde relieved 9th Bde Sigs OK	
12 am	6th Div took over all lines.	

121/6306

38th Division

28th Signal Coy
Vol XII

Secret.

War Diary

28th Div Signal Co R.E.

June 1915

Sheet
Square
H 7 C.
6 am.

Fine
6th Division taken over at midnight

9 am
1-6-15

Coy route march to WATOU to
rest camp. DHQ. here also.
Lines laid to HERZEELE to
84th Bde.
Installed phone to 5th Corps RA
RE & G.S.

7 pm
WATOU

Seven men on leave to England.

2.6.15
9 am

Fine NE gusty
Sigs OK
Line laid to WINIZEELE for
83rd Bde & HOUTKERQUE for
85th Bde

7 pm

Fourth detachment arrived from
Reserve Coy in England comprising
1 Officer 32 ORs 1 Cable waggon
1 GS waggon 1 limbered RE
17 horses 6 cycles & two motorcycles

3.6.15
9 am

Fine
Sigs OK.
Equipment all being overhauled
& waggons cleaned

4.6.15	Fine
9 am	Sigs OK
	Communication with 83rd & 84th Bdes direct
	Sounder to 8th Corps & 2nd Army
	Phone to 5th & 6th Corps
2 pm	Despatched (Requear) 4th det to 2nd Army 17 ORs 1 cable & 1 tendered RE waggon
5.6.15	Fine
9 am	Sigs OK
	Technical Stores checking & overhauling
6.6.15	Fine
	Sigs OK
7.6.15	Fine
	Sigs OK
8.6.15	Fine morning heavy thunderstorm afternoon
9 am	Sigs OK
3 pm	85th Bde on HOUTKERQUE lines
9.6.15	Fine dull
9 am	Sigs OK

10.6.15	Rainy
9 am	Sigs. OK
11.6.15	Fine
9 am	Sigs. OK
	84th Bde off line at HERZEELE
12.6.15	Fine N wind
9 am	Sigs OK
	Line HERZEELE – HOUTKERQUE
	picked up.
13.6.15	Fine
9 am	Sigs. OK
3 pm	Visited WESTOUTRE to see
	14th Div Sigs re taking over.
14.6.15	Fine
8 am	Party left to take over from 14th Div.
9 am	Coy route march to WATOU
	Sigs left at WATOU to 2nd Corps
	& 5th Corps 83rd & 85th Bdes
	all phones & other lines cleared
11 am	DHQ to WESTOUTRE
	14th Div comms taken over.
6 pm	83rd & 85th Bdes thro 2nd Corps.
	FRA

WESTOUTRE	Fine
15.6.15	Coy in bivouacs in field S of village
9 am.	Sigs OK
	~~Line laid to SCHERPENBERG from report centre~~
9.30 am	RC opened 420 C
3 pm	RC closed
16.6.15	Fine N wind
9 am.	Sigs OK
9.30 am	RC opened
2 pm	RC closed
17.6.15	Fine N wind
9 am	Sigs OK
9.30 am	RC opened
2 pm	RC closed
18.6.15	Fine NE wind
9 am	Sigs OK
10 am	RC lines taken over from 4th RA
19.6.15	Fine
9 am	Sigs OK
	New line laid from LACLYTE to KEMMEL for 83rd Bde HQ &
4 pm	new direct line to Summer Capt Bradley left to join 4th Division Signals
9 pm	new lines OK

20.6.15		Fine
9 am		Sigs. OK. to 83rd & 84th Bdes. 85th Bde via 2nd Corps
4.15 pm		85th Bde in. covered in line to LACLYTE
21.6.15		Fine
9 am		Sigs. OK to all brigades
10 am		LT. WRIGHT reported for duty
22.6.15		Fine
9 am		Sigs. OK
		Phone lines being constructed.
23.6.15		Fine
9 am		Sigs OK
		Line being constructed to SCHERPENBURG for report centre Lines to ola R.C.H 20 C handed over to 85th bde as lprs. 83rd Bde hq. to LACLYTE new lines being laid
24.6.15		Fine
9 am		Sigs OK
4 pm		new lines to 83rd HQ Sounders telephones OK.
11.15 pm		83rd Bde at LACLYTE

25.6.15	Rain	
9 am	Sig. OK	
10 am	R.C. opened	
3.50 pm	Line to 83rd 84th & 85th all fused by lightning	
7 pm	All lines OK. And lightning discharger board fitted. Lines in places fused	
26.6.15	Fine	
9 am	Sig. OK	
27.6.15	Fine dull later showery	
9 am	Sig. OK except sounder to 85th	
10 am	85th Line OK breakage caused by observation balloon	
8 pm	New Comsac airline completion to 83rd Bde	
28.6.15	Dull showers	
9 am	Sig. OK	
29.6.15	Dull showery	
9 am	Sig. OK	
30.6.15	Fine some showers	
9 am	Sig. OK	

121/6390.

28th Division

98th Signal Coy

Vol XIII

Diary

28th Divl Signal Co.

July 1915

WESTOUTRE

1.7.15	Dull some showers.	
9 am	Sigs OK.	
2.7.15	Fine	
	Sigs OK.	
3.7.15	Fine	
	Sigs OK	
9 am	Commenced buried D5 cable & enamelled wire from 84th Bde HQ H32 to battle hq. ~~H77~~ H106	
9 pm	Party working on above on exposed portion 500ˣ complete.	
4.7.15	Fine	
9 am	Sigs OK.	
	Commenced buried D5 & enamelled wire from KEMMEL back 250ˣ complete	
9 pm	Party on 84th buried lines 500ˣ complete	
5.7.15	Fine	
9 am	Sigs OK	
	Party on KEMMEL buried lines	
9 pm	Party on 84th buried line	
6.7.15	Fine	
9 am	Sigs OK	
	Parties on both buried lines	

7.7.15	Fine
9 am	Sigs OK.
	Parties on buried lines
8.7.15	Fine
9 am	Sigs OK.
	Parties on buried lines
9.7.15	Fine
9 am	Sigs OK
	Parties on buried lines
10.7.15	Fine
9 am	Sigs OK
	Buried lines to KEMMEL HILL
	completed & tested OK
11 am	One NCO & one Sapper to GHQ
	wireless for instructions
	Buried line to 80th Advanced
	completed & tested OK
	500ˣ remain to be done to 80th deles
11.7.15	Fine dull
9 am	Sigs OK
12.7.15	Fine
9 am	Sigs OK
	Lt ESCOMBE to 83rd bde. Lt PERKINS
	sick.

13.7.15	Fine	
9 am	Sigs OK	
	Visited 50th Div. re taking over two brigade front.	
14.7.15	Fine	
9 am	Sigs OK	
8 pm	9th Bde taken over 84th.	
	84th Bde to LOCRE	
	Very wet nights	
15.7.15	Fine	
9 am	Sigs OK.	
10 am	88th Bde moved to LOCRE	
3.30 pm	84th Bde moving to KEMMEL	
6.15 pm	Ditto opened office	
16.7.15	Fine wet night	
9 am	Sigs OK.	
	83rd Bde LACLYTE SC & telephone	
	84th Bde KEMMEL Vibrator	
	88th Bde LOCRE Vibrator	
9.30 pm	88th Bde left LOCRE	
10.15 pm	Ditto opened office DRANOUTRE	
	SC & telephones	

17.7	Rain showers. Very windy
9 am	Sigs. OK.
10 am	Considerable breaking lines by small bobbins of last consignment smashing up.
5 pm	All lines OK
18.7.15	Bright wind gusty
9 am	Sigs. OK.
11.25	83rd line full earth.
12 nt	Ditto OK.
12.30	84th telephone dis
1.3	Ditto OK
2.45 pm	R.C telephone dis
4.15 pm	Ditto OK. wire rusted through at binding on permanent pole.
19.7.15	Fine
9 am	Sigs OK
8.35 am	Sounder line 2nd Corps bad
9.5 am	Sigs OK
20.7.15	Fine
9 am	Sigs OK. Major Saunders on leave
1.40 pm	85th Bde dis - 3 poles dragged down by balloons.

21.7.15	Fine	
9 am	Sigs OK	
10 am	50th Div off line (moving)	
22.7.15	Fine	
9 am	Sigs OK	
	Laying new lines for CRA move	
	to M 20 c.	
	LT. ESCOMB returned, LT PERKINS to duty	
23.7.15	Fine rain during night	
9 am	Sigs OK.	
	new lines for CRA completed	
4.25 pm	CRA in new position	
	Sigs OK.	
24.7.15	Fine	
9 am	Sigs OK	
25.7.15	Fine	
4 am	Major Saunders returned from leave	
9 am	Sigs OK	
10.45 am	17th Division on left in Commn	
26.7.15	Showery	
9 am	Sigs OK	
10.15 am	84th T. lines dis	
1.45 pm	Above OK broken by Shrapnel	

27.7	Fine	
9 am	Sigs OK	Messages
8 pm	R E park on phone exchange	494
28.7.15	Very showery	Messages
9 am	Sigs OK	471
	Commenced D5 line on river &	
	lend metallic line buried from	
	85th Bde. T3b.	
29.7.15	Fine	
9 am	Sigs OK	
bet. 4 & 5 pm	All lines to 84th bde cut thro'	Messages
	retaliation of Germans by 9.2	486
	firing	
5.20 pm	Sigs OK.	
	Parties on buried lines 85th.	
30.7.15	Fine	
9 am	Sigs OK	
	Parties on buried lines 85th.	Messages
		536
31.7.15	Fine	
9 am	Sigs OK.	
	Parties on buried lines 85th Bde.	Messages
		534

LOCRE TOUTRE

1.7.15   Dull some showers.
9 am.   Sigs OK.

2.7.15   Fine.
               Sigs OK.

3.7.15   Fine
               Sigs OK
9 am   Commenced buried D5 cable & enamelled
               wire from 84th Bde HQ. H.22.b to
               battle hq. H.106
9 pm   Party working on above on exposed
               portion.   500° complete

4.7.15   Fine
9 am   Sigs OK.
               Commenced buried D5 & enamelled
               wire from KEMMEL back. 250° complete
9 pm   Party on 84th buried line 500° complete

5.7.15   Fine
9 am   Sigs OK
               Party on KEMMEL buried line
9 pm   Party on 84th buried line

6.7.15   Fine
9 am.   Sigs OK.
               Parties on both buried lines

2.

7.7.15 9 am	Fine Sigs OK. Parties on buried lines	
8.7.15 9 am	Fine Report OK Parties on buried lines	
9.7.15 9 am	Fine Sigs OK Parties on buried lines	
10.7.15 9 am 11 am	Fine Report OK Buried lines to KEMMEL HILL completed & tested OK. One NCO & one sapper to GHQ needed for construction Buried line to 84th Armoured completed & tested OK. 500' remain to be done to 85th ditto	
11.7.15 9 am	Fine dull Report OK	
12.7.15 9 am	Fine Report OK. Lt ESCOMBE to 13th Div. Lt PERKINS ditto	

3.

13.7.15   Fine
9 am   Sigs OK
     Printed 50th Div. is taking over two
     brigade front.

14.7.15   Fine
9 am   Sigs OK
8 pm   6th Bde taken over 84th
     84th Bde to LOCRE
     Very wet night

15.7.15   Fine
9 am   Sigs OK.
10 am   85th Bde moved to LOCRE
6.30 pm   84th Bde moving to KEMMEL
6.45 pm   Ditto opened office

16.7.15   Fine   wet night
9 am   Sigs. OK.
     63rd Bde   LOCLITE   Sc & telephone
     84th Bde   KEMMEL   Vibrator
     85th Bde   LOCRE   Vibrator
9.30 pm   85th Bde left LOCRE
10.15 pm   Ditto opened office DRANOUTRE
              Sc & telephone

17.7.15	Rain showers Boy windy	
9 am	Sigs OK	
10 am	Immovable breaking lines by	
	Sappers taking of land comm[unication]	
	making up	
5 pm	all lines OK	
18.7.15	Bright warm sunny	
9 am	Sigs OK	
11.25	B" line full earth	
12.24	ditto OK	
12.30	B" telephone dis	
1.3	ditto OK	
2.45 pm	R.C. telephone dis	
10.15	ditto OK more trouble	
	trying a breaking or permanent	
	poles	
19.7.15	Fine	
9 am	Sigs OK	
1.35	Stranded line 3rd Corps line	
9.0 pm	Sigs OK	
20.7.15	Fine	
9 am	Sigs OK Major Stanmore sees on lines	
1.45 pm	16th Bav gun 3 shells Sanggart	
	aimed by trenches	

		5

21.7.15   Fine
9 am   Sig. OK
10 am   50th Div. Off line (moving)

22.7.15 Fine
9 am   Report OK
         Laying new lines for C R A move
         to M 20 C.
         LT. ESCOMB returned, LT PERKINS to duty

23.7.15 Fine   rain during night
9 am   Report OK
         New lines for C R A completing
4.25 pm C R A in new position
         Report OK.

24.7.15 Fine
9 am   Report OK

25.7.15 Fine
6 am   Major Sanderson returned from leave
9 am   Report OK
10.0 am 7th Divisn on left relieved

26.7.15 Showery
9 am

28th Division

121/6874

War Diary

28th Divl Signal Co RE

August 1915

Vol IX

War Diary   28th Divl Signal Co. R.E.

1.8.15 HESTOUTRE 9 am	Fine Sigs OK Lines in river & buried D5 to 85th Bde completing tested OK Lt Parsons on leave	Messages 524
2.8.15 9 am	Fine Sigs OK Completing lead covered metallic buried line.	Messages 543
3.8.15 9 am	Fine Sigs OK	Messages 592
4.8.15 9 am	Fine Sigs OK Commenced new trunk line of comic airline on H poles.	Messages 487
5.8.15 9 am	Fine Sigs OK	Messages 434
6.8.15 4 am 9 am 3 pm	Fine Lt Parsons returned Sigs OK Went CAESTRE see 37th Sig. re training	Messages 598

7.8.15	Fine	
9am	Sigs OK	
	Two wireless sets sent to 6th Div at request 2nd Army.	Messages 522
	Burrows nettalie + D5 completion to 83rd Bde new hq. M18 d	
	Parties erecting new trunk airlines	
	St DeSalis. 85th Bde Sig. on leave.	
8.8.15	Fine Gusty	
9am	Sigs OK.	
10 am	Spare line run into LOCREHOF for 110th Bde	
	One light draught horse died during night. PM this morning	
4.30pm	110th Bde in circuit	
	New aux line completed	
	picking up nettalie to 83rd Bde M 18 d.	Messages 558
9.8.15	Fine thundery forenoon.	
9 am	Sigs OK	
	Continuing construction aux lines	
4 pm	Major Bannerman &c Sigs ? 6 OR. 37th Sqdn arrived for attachment	Messages 619

10.8.15 9 am	Fine Sigs. OK. Commenced buried metallic lead covered & D5 cables from 84th Bde to 84th Bde. Major Saunders A/ay successfully took cables through culverts 40 & 20 yards long on route. Airline routes completing	Messages 610
11.8.15 9 am	Fine Sigs. OK. South route of air lines completed & 85th Bde buried lines picked up. Metallic circuit to 83rd Bde complete. Parties on burying metallic phone & D5 vibrator lines 85th to 84th bdes.	Messages 633
12.8.15 9 am 6 pm	Fine Sigs. OK Major Bannerman 5/ Sig. returned when first remainder staying	Messages 654

13.8.15	Showery.	
9 am	Sigs OK	
1 pm	Sounder on metallic circuit to 83rd Bde new HQ. OK.	
3.30 pm	83rd Bde to new HQ	
8 pm	Party working on buried line where exposed.	Messages 563
14.8.15	Fine	
9 am	Sigs OK	
12 noon	St FORBES & 7 men 37th Signals arrived for attachment	
2.30 pm	First party with Lt SLINGO returned to CAESTRE	Messages 714
15.8.15	Fine Showery	
9 am	Sigs OK	
3 pm	Report centre opens Sigs OK.	
5 pm	Report centre closed Metallic telephone completed to 84th Bde.	Messages 673
16.8.15	Fine Thundery	
9 am	Sigs OK.	
	Metallic phone giving lot of trouble - lineman on it	Messages 572

17.8.15	Fine early. Thunder & heavy showers	
9 am	Sigs OK.	
	Metallic phone 84th & 85th Bdes faulty.	
11 am	Span down - disturbed test box twice, badly crossed.	Message 554
4 pm	Phone OK.	
18.8.15	Fine	
9 am	Sigs OK.	
	CAPT. PERKINS on leave.	Message 596.
	Constant trouble with new pattern phone at Bdes through Staff not replacing receiver.	
19.8.15	Fine	
9 am	Sigs OK.	
	Phone line 84th & 85th dis - iron wire on airline not standing strain of spans	
9.30 am	Above OK	Message 526.

20.8.15 9am	Fine Sigs OK Detachments out reeling up all unmarked cables.	Messages 570
21.8.15 9am	Rain Sigs OK One Officer 7 men returned to 37th Signal Co. Eight men reported LT. KIRBY on leave	Messages Sent 333 Transmitted 31 Received 140 504
22.8.15 9am	Fine Showers. Sigs OK	Messages Sent 317 Transd. 41 Recd. 123 481
23.8.15 9am	Dull Sigs OK Corpl Lee of No 3 Section killed	Messages. Sent 323 Trans 38 Recd 142 503

24.8.15		Dull	
9 am		Sigs OK	
		Capt. Perkins returned from leave	Messages
		Airlines much disturbed by	Sig Rey. 323
		civilians collecting crops.	Trans. 26
5 pm		R A digging party dug through	Rcd. 139
		lead & D5 cable to 85th Bde.	488
		Report sent G Staff.	
		All men 37th Sig Co returned to	
		unit	
25.8.15		Fine	Messages
9 am		Sigs OK	Sent 307
		Airlines again in contact	Trans. 25
		caused by loaded waggons of	Rcd. 153
		civilians	485
		Asked CRA that correct map showing	
		any proposed lines be submitted	
		before commencing digging	
26.8.15		Fine	
9 am		Sigs OK	
		Buried lines at 85th Dugout being	Messages
		relaid where destroyed by R.A	Sent 300
		digging party	Trans. 19
5 pm.		Electric light lorry arrived	Rcd. 140
			459

27.8.15	Fine	Messages	
9 am	Sigs OK	Sent	353
	Electric light installed. very	Stations	26
	successful.	Recd	148
	2 D Horses supplied		527
28.8.15	Fine	Messages	
9 am	Sigs OK.	Sent	316
	Lt. ESCOMBE on leave.	Stations	27
	LT. KIRBY returned from leave	Recd	143
			486
		Messages	
29.8.15	Fine dull. rain later	Sent	278
9 am	Sigs OK.	Stations	16
10 am	Airlines in contact, requiring	Recd	134
	shortening of spans & spreaders		428
	due to wind		
12 noon	24 men of 84th Bde reported for		
	course buzzer instruction		

30.8.15 9 am	Showery Sig OK Constructed Signal lines to Cavalry Corps & French lines around communications	Messages Sent 276 Trans 12 Recd 112 400
31.8.15 9 am	Dull Showery. Sig OK Rebuilding comic airline routes to R A at LOCRE chateau.	Messages. Sent. 263 Trans 26 Recd 148 437

W Saunders
Major
O C. 28th Divl Signal Co R E

Volume No. 1

MEDITERRANEAN EXPEDITIONARY FORCE.

WAR DIARY.

Unit 28th Div Signal Co

From 1.9.15   To 30.9.15

War Diary

of

28th Divl Signal Co R.E.

September 1915

Date Hour Place	Summary of Events & Information	Remarks
WESTOUTRE 1.9.15	Fair showery later	
9 am	Signals OK.	
2 pm	Sent one man on months leave on signing on for termination of war.	Messages Sent 334 Trans 29
6 pm	R.A. phone rebt on new route	Recd 133 496
2.9.15	Fair	Messages
9 am	Sigs OK	Sent 338
5 pm	Heavy rain	Trans 32 Recd 138 508
3.9.15	Heavy rain all day.	Messages
9 am	Sig OK	Sent 343
	S/ ESCOMB returned from leave	Trans 30 Recd 138 511
4.9.15	Dull Some rain	
9 am	Sig OK	
5.30 pm	Received instructions 2nd Army to send extra officer to 46th Div	
7.30	S/ ESCOMB to 46th Div	

		Messages.
4.9.15	contd	Sent 314
7.5pm	Dis on buried line to 84th Bde in ditch of road N19C faulty	Issues 36
11.10pm	100ˣ bridged over temporarily	Recd. 123
		473

		Messages.
5.9.15	Bright	Sent 291
9am	Sigs OK.	Issues 23
	Lt. Hibb on leave.	Recd 136
	Sent M.C. to ABBEVILLE to get roller bearing for Singer car – on indent 3 weeks – Found plenty in stock.	450
11 am	G.O.C. inspected camp.	

		Messages.
6.9.15	Fine	Sent 295
9am	Sigs OK	Issues 17
	Completing lines to R.C. augusts SCHERPENBERG. which was shelled during morning.	Recd 130
		442

		Messages.
7.9.15	Fine	Sent 321
9am	Sigs OK	Issues 29
9.30pm	2/Lieut G Rooke reported for duty.	Recd 121
		471

8.9.15 9 am	Fine Sigs OK Singer car again running & very noisy, artillery reports badly strained; report sent abod M.T. Metallic telephone line to 84th & 85th giving trouble (earthy). Lines tested to Adv. 83rd Bde & found OK with connection thro'	Messages Sent 313 Ceans 19 Recd 143 475
9.9.15 9 am	Fine Sigs OK. except phone (84th & 85th) due to spirit soldered joints eating through.	Messages Sent 286 Ceans 20 Recd 114 420
10.9.15 9 am	Fine Sigs OK	Messages Sent 335 Ceans 22 Recd 116 473
11.9.15 9 am	Fine Sigs OK Lt. Hill returned from leave.	Messages Sent 290 Ceans 26 Recd 123 439

12.9.15 9 am	Fine Sigs OK Visited all C trenches of 85th Bde.	Messages. Sent 307 Seads 22 Recd 151 480
13.9.15 9 am 12.15 pm 4.30 pm	Fine Sigs OK Mellalie received 85th Bde dis cow in ditch having broken line Line OK Car (Singer) sent to 28th Supply column, gears back axle.	Messages. Sent 295 Seads 40 Recd 125 460
14.9.15 9 am	Dull showery Sigs OK	Messages Sent 309 Seads 29 Recd 128 466
15.9.15 9 am 3 pm	Fine Sigs OK D.A.S visited HQrs.	Messages. Sent 297 Seads 41 Recd. 142 480

16.9.15 9 am	Fine Sigs OK		Messages. Sent 373 Trans 40 Recd. 144 557
17.9.15 9 am	Fine Sigs. OK		Messages Sent 368 Trans 33 Recd 154 555
18.9.15 9 am 10 am	Fine Sigs OK Sigs 2nd Canadian Div. called re arranging take over.		Messages Sent 324 Trans 33 Recd 135 492
19.9.15 9 am	Fine Sigs OK Bde Officers Canadians with Line taking over lines 2 Sergts 6 men Canadians with HQrs.		Messages Sent 346 Trans 66 Recd 181 593

20.9.15	Fine	
9 am	Sigs OK.	
	One cable detachment to MERRIS installing lines to 2nd Corps & new bde billetting areas	
4 pm	Line from MERRIS through to 2nd Corps.	
5.30 pm	Buried line to 84th Bde dis - two working party cutting through it.	Messages. Sent 386. Trans 110 Recd 183 679
6.30 pm	Above OK	
9.30 pm	84th Bde handed over to 3rd Canadian Bde.	
	84th Bde at LOCRE	
21.9.15	Fine	
9 am	Sigs OK.	Messages
	84th Bde closed office LOCRE	Sent 409
1.25 pm	84th Bde in communication from PRADELLES.	Trans 141 Recd 171 721
7.30 pm	85th Bde Sigs relieved by 4th Canadian Sigs.	
	85th Bde opened at DRANOUTRE	
22.9.15	Fine	Messages
9 am	Sigs OK.	Sent 502
1.30 pm	85th Bde opened at STRAZEELE	Trans 157
10 pm	5th Canadian Bde relieved 83rd Bde.	Recd 192 851

WESTOUTRE 23.9.15			
6 am	Coy marched off to MERRIS.		
9 am	Sigs OK		
	Completion of relief D.R. by Canadians.	Messages	
	All communications handed over.	Sent	359
MERRIS	Office open as DHQ.	Trans	28
9.30 am	Coy arrived MERRIS	Recd	118
	Took over billets for 70 men		505
	Mounted men & horses in field.		
1.30 pm	83rd on line at OULTERSTEENE		
24.9.15	Wet night, bright midday	Messages	
9 am	Rigs OK	Sent	323
		Trans	20
		Recd	138
			481
25.9.15	Wet night		
9 am	Sigs OK		
9.45 am	Commenced wire to 3rd Corps HQ.	Messages 511	
10.20 am	Recd. wire 3rd Corps offering wires		
	Cancelled detachment running lines.		
1 pm	Through to 3rd Corps IRC		

MERRIS 26.9.15	Fine	
7 am	Sigs OK. Office closed.	
MERVILLE	Office opened.	
7 am	Coy moving by march route	
	O cable sections reported	
	from 2nd Corps.	
BETHUNE	Office opened.	
4.30 pm	Direct line 1st Army.	hot through
	Phone line through 2nd Div.	
	84th Bde communicating via	Messages 232.
	1st Army. from PARADIS.	
10 pm	Line laid to 83rd at ROBECQ	
	85th Bde in BETHUNE (orderly)	
8 pm	Coy arrived & billeted	

BETHUNE 27.9.15	Fine.	
12.40 am	Line to 1st Army OK.	
9 am	Sigs OK.	
9.30 am	84th closed office PARADIS.	
	Bde moving to BETHUNE	
4 pm	R.C. open. SAILLY LABOURSE	
	85th forward on line from	
	9th Div.	
	Constant trouble with enemy	
	of new line from old 36th	
	Bde HQrs.	
8 pm	Sigs OK to BETHUNE & bde	

SAILLY
LAHOURSE

28.9.15	Line	
6 am	Sig. OK	
~~6 p~~	Office taken over from	Messages
	8th Div.	Sent 402
	Line to 84th Bde. SAILLY and	Trans 77
	83rd Bde NOYELLES.	Rec'd 171
11.55 pm	Line to Corps. earthing	650

29.9.15	Mist all day	
3.50 am	Corps line OK	
9 am	Sig. OK	Messages
12.15 pm	83rd Bde moved forward	Sent 363
	to new HQrs leaving Staff	Trans 53
	Capt. on line as intermediate	Rec'd 297
2.27 pm	84th closed office moving	713
5.50 pm	84th reopened ANNEQUIN	
10.40 pm	WC set from YBd removed	

30.9.15	Line	
9 am	Sig. OK at both offices.	
~~9~~	~~strikethrough~~	
~~	~~strikethrough~~	
~~	~~strikethrough~~	
5.55 pm	84th closed office - Messages	
	sent to 88th to await arrival	

| 6 pm ~~3.30pm~~ | Contacts on Corps lines | Messages Sent 522 Issues 62 Recd 293 ——— 877 |

H C Saunders / Major
OC 28th Signal Co R.E.

Volume No. 2

MEDITERRANEAN EXPEDITIONARY FORCE.

WAR DIARY.

Unit 28th Div Signal Co

From 1.10.15   To 30.10.15

War Diary

of

28th Divl Signal Co R.E.

October 1915

SAILLY			
LABOURSE			
1.10.15	Rainy		
9.55 am	85th relieved by 84th		
	85th on line ANNEQUIN		
4.40 pm	85th Bde closed moving	Messages	
6.8 pm	83rd Bde relieved by 84th Bde	Sent	570
6.20 pm	88th Bde reopened BEUVRY	Trans	36
	intermediate on BETHUNE	Recd	250
	line		856
8.40 pm	83rd Bde closed office		
5.0 pm	boy arrived by march		
7 am	RA moved from BETHUNE		
12 noon	RA sigs taken from 9th Div		
2.10.15	Fine		
9 am	Sigs OK		
	Signals to 84th Bde maintained	Messages	
	2 detachments working in lines	Sent	538
	in trenches up to Bde hqrs	Trans	37
	Received instructions from Corps	Recd	250
	re lamp signals arranged		825
	with Bde section		
8 pm	Heavy fighting		
	Lamp signals sent but not		
	observed at FOSSE 9.		

3.10.15	Line	
9 am	Sig. OK	
	84th Bde in action	
11 am	Line dis to 84th above last test station	
11.20 am	Sig. OK. 84th	
11 am	46th Div opened office BETHUNE notified us	
1 pm	83rd Bde closed at BEUVRY and reopened ANNEQUIN same time	
1.40–2.15	Staff speaking to 84th Bde delaying SB messages	
6 pm	New station open CLARKS KEEP for Staff Captain 84 & 83 Bdes.	
8 pm	Sig. bad to 84th Bde	
	83rd relieving 84th.	
9 pm	Sig. good to 83rd	
10.30 pm	84th Bde arrived CLARKS KEEP	
10.35 pm	D.R. reported loss role maps from 1st Corps to DHQ. 1st Corps informed duplicate sent.	Messages Sent 451 Trans 116 Recd. 227 — 794
11.55 pm	Above received	

4.10.15	Fine	
9.20 am	~~2nd Bde~~ Sigs OK	Messages
	Guards div. relieved 2nd Div	Sent 451
	Call changed to GDR	Trans 94
		Recd 245
		790
10 am	Signals OK	
5.10.15	Fine early then wet	
8 am	Line to Guards Div dis	
	fault in their office	
8.35 am	88th Bde closed office at CLARKS KEEP	
10 am	84th Bde at ANNEQUIN	Messages
10.35 am	85th Bde ditto	Sent 509
2 pm to 4 pm	83rd Bde & G. Staff using line	Trans 184
	for speaking much delay on	Recd 148
	messages	841
6 pm	84th Bde moving BETHUNE	
6.30 pm	Line dis to 88th Bde —	
	omnibus carried line away	
7 pm	Thro to 88th Bde	
7.30 pm	New line from pump test	
	station to Central Bayou	
	completed. Good Sigs	

6.10.15	Fine	
8 am	Sig. OK	
	Lineman at test stations	
	relieved by Guards signals	
9.45 am	Handing over to Guards Div	
10.20 am	Office closed at SAILLY LABOURSE	
	Office opened at BUSNES	
	same hour	
~~2.15p~~	~~Having~~ Coy marched from SAILLY LABOURSE to BUSNES.	~~Messages~~
10 am	Office closed in BETHUNE	
2.18 pm	Through to 1st Corps on S.C. set & telephones	Horses & wagons in field. Men in Barn. HQrs & DRS in Stables attached Chateau of D.H.Q.
5 pm	Communications by wire to 84th Bde at BUSNES district	
6 pm	Coy arrived BUSNES.	Messages
8.20 pm	Ditto 88th Bde at L'ECLEME	Sent 167 Leans 17
10.37 pm	Ditto 83rd Bde at GONNEHEM.	Recd. 84
		268

BUSNES

7.10.15	Fine		
9 am	Sigs OK	Messages	
10.55 am	Phone line complete to 84th Bde	Sent	339
4.50 pm	do 85th "	Jeans	10
7.45 pm	do 83rd "	Recd	145
			494

8.10.15	Fine	Messages	
7.30 am	Sigs OK	Sent	340
	All differences being listed	Jeans	20
	& indented for.	Recd	118
			478

9.10.15	Dull but no rain	Messages	
8 am	Sigs OK	Sent	315
	Visited SAILLY LABOURSE to	Jeans	16
	see HQ. R.A. Sigs OK	Recd	133
			464

10.10.15	Dull		
9 am	Sigs OK	Messages	
	HQrs signallers out for practice	Sent	246
	with Bde signallers. Helio flag.	Jeans	28
6 pm	All signallers inst lamp.	Recd	110
			384

11-10-15	Dull	Messages
8 am	Sig OK	Sent 277
	Signallers training	Trans 22
		Recd 113
		417
12-10-15	Dull no rain	Messages
8 am	Sig OK	Sent 327
		Trans 19
		Recd 122
		468
13-10-15	Dull no rain	Messages
8 am	Sig OK	Sent 150
		Trans 24
		Recd 294
		468
14.10.15	Dull	Messages
	Sig OK.	Sent 130
		Trans 20
		Recd 285
		435

15.10.15	Dull.	Messages
8 am	Sig. OK	Sent 258
3.39 pm	83rd moved to BEUVRY.	Trans. 8
6.30 pm	Messages to 83rd through 7th Div.	Recd 134
		427
16.10.15	Dull	Messages
8 am	Sig. OK	Sent 344
12.45 pm	2/5 Bde working through	Trans 23
	83rd Bde's late Office	Recd 160
		527
17.10.15	Dull	
8 am	Sig. OK	
8.40 am	85th closing office moving to	Messages
	AIELETTE	Sent 220
4 pm	Office closed BUSNES &	Trans 71
	reopened at LE QUESNOY.	Recd 98
	(Working to 85th via 2nd Div.	389
	(" 84th via 7th Div.	
	(" 83rd direct	
	A&Q work to 2nd Div. at	
	BETHUNE	

18.10.15		Fine	
8 am		Sig OK Office moving	Messages
		with DHQ to BETHUNE	Sent 457
		84th Bde moved from BUSNES	Trans 101
		to AVELETTE work by D.R.	Recd 177
			735
5pm		Direct line BETHUNE to	
		Corps. lines LEQUESNOY	
		hewn spare.	
19.10.15		Fine	Messages
8 am		Sig. OK	Sent 572
9 am		All coy moved to BETHUNE	Trans 91
12.10 pm		Communication	Recd 208
		established 85th Bde N of canal	871
3.40 pm		LEQUESNOY. Office closed.	
		two operators & phone exchange	
		now working here.	
20.10.15		Fine	
8 am		Sig OK	Messages
12.20 pm		20th Bde relieved 85th Bde N	Sent 500
		of canal.	Trans 69
4.2 pm		85th Bde closed	Recd 236
11.20 pm		85th Bde brought in line at	805
		HINGETTE	

21.10.15	Drill	
8 am	Sig. ok	
10.20 am	Office handed over to 7th Div.	
12.30 pm	Coy marched to LILLERS station & entrained.	
22.10.15	Fine In train	
23.10.15	Fine In train	
MARSEILLES		
24.10.15	Fine	
1.30 am	Arrived MARSEILLES. marched to camp. PARC DE BORELY.	
25.10.15	~~Drill~~ rain. 6 D.R.S embarked with DHQ.	
26.10.15	Rain all day.	
27.10.15	Drill.	
28.10.15	Fine	

29.10.15	Fine
30.10.15	Dull wet. L. BRIGDEN & 7 ORs embarked H.T. KAROA with 7 cycles & 1 M Cycle.

H Chambers
Major
OC. 28th Signal Co RE.

www.ingramcontent.com/pod-product-compliance
Lightning Source LLC
Chambersburg PA
CBHW081543160426
43191CB00011B/1826